P9-DDI-121

DISCARD

Safari Beneath the Sea

The Wonder World of the North Pacific Coast

Diane Swanson

Photographs by the
Royal British Columbia Museum

Sierra Club Books for Children

San Francisco

The Sierra Club, founded in 1892 by John Muir, has devoted itself to the study and protection of the earth's scenic and ecological resources—mountains, wetlands, woodlands, wild shores and rivers, deserts and plains. The publishing program of the Sierra Club offers books to the public as a nonprofit educational service in the hope that they may enlarge the public's understanding of the Club's basic concerns. The Sierra Club has some sixty chapters in the United States and in Canada. For information about how you may participate in its programs to preserve wilderness and the quality of life, please address inquiries to Sierra Club, 730 Polk Street, San Francisco, CA 94109.

First U.S. Edition

First published in Canada by Whitecap Books Ltd., 1086 West 3rd Street,
North Vancouver, British Columbia V7P 3J6

All photographs (including cover) by the Royal British Columbia Museum, except the following: pages 46, 48 and 55 by Jim Borrowman; page 37 by Phil Edgell; page 4 by Colleen MacMillan; and pages 39 and 42 by Neil McDaniel.

Cover design by Warren Clark
Interior design and typesetting by Margaret Ng
Printed in Canada

10 9 8 7 6 5 4 3 2 1

Library of Congress Cataloging-in-Publication data is available from Sierra Club Books for Children, 100 Bush Street, 13th Floor, San Francisco, California 94104.

Contents

Acknowledgments

My warmest thanks go to the following for their assistance in producing this book:

- Jim Cosgrove, Phil Lambert and Alex Peden, all of the Royal British Columbia Museum, for their sound scientific advice;

- the SAFARI team (who took thousands of children on two award-winning, high-tech adventures along the magnificent North Pacific coast), especially Brent Cooke, Roger Frampton, Bernice Mittertreiner and Susan Wilkey, for inspiration; and

- Wayne, Timothy and Carolyn Swanson, my terrific family, for all their help in getting this manuscript through its final stages after I broke my leg.

Chapter One

North Pacific Wonder World

Many kinds of jelly-fish have delicate, see-through bodies.

I magine fish that tie themselves in knots, plants that flash lights in the dark, sea stars that turn their stomachs inside out and mammals that hammer their food. Life in the sea is bizarre, beautiful, funny and fabulous. And there's more of it in the cold waters off British Columbia, Washington, Oregon and Southeast Alaska than almost anywhere else in the world.

But that's not surprising. The cold waters of this North Pacific sea are very rich in nutrients that help plants grow. From as deep as 1,000 feet, water loaded with nutrients rises to replace surface water moved by winds and currents. And rivers carry even more nutri-

ents to the sea. The result is a lush "pasture" of plants that attracts a lot of animals.

Different kinds of sea life live in different kinds of places: deep and shallow, rocky and sandy, covered and bare. Some prefer relatively quiet waters in narrow inlets or along coasts sheltered by islands. Others live best in wild waters along coasts exposed to the ocean or in narrow, current-swept passages. The coastal North Pacific has it all.

Shaped like an ostrich feather, the orange sea pen anchors itself to the sea floor with its foot.

At Home in Quiet Waters

Life in calm inlets is less varied than in other waters, but it is often abundant. In some places, sea stars gather so thickly that they bury underwater walls with their orange and purple bodies. Sea grasses and seaweeds cluster in shallow water, and masses of throbbing jellyfish drift in gentle flows near the surface.

The deeper water of inlets is home to strange creatures, such as skinny feather stars that color whole slopes a fluffy, pale yellow. Below them, yellow and white cloud sponges, up to 100 years old, grow in large numbers and huge sizes—to more than 6 feet across. Still deeper, gorgonian coral grows in many graceful fans of red and orange more than 3 feet high.

Where islands shield the water from the ocean's blasts, many more kinds of sea life appear. Bright-eyed seals bob up and down in harbors and noisy sea lions haul themselves onto rocks in winter. They chase after fish, especially thousands of herring that swarm to the shallows to lay and fertilize their eggs.

Many "soft creatures" live here, too. Plumelike worms, sponges and other small animals coat pilings of piers. On sandy sea floors, crowds of featherlike orange sea pens capture food delivered by currents. And in dens among rocks and reefs, big octopuses crack open crabs to feed.

At Home in Wild Waters

On coasts exposed to the ocean, sea life faces waves, winds and currents strong enough to carve caves in rocky shores. But the top layer of this wild sea also stirs up a rich supply of food. It's a great place to live—for anything that can avoid being crushed, scoured or whisked away. In fact, much sea life thrives here and grows to

Where Giants Live

The cool, food-rich waters of the North Pacific make good growing grounds for giants. Because there is so much food, most animals don't need to use a lot of energy to get their meals. Some kinds of North Pacific animals are the biggest in the world: the giant Pacific octopus, the red sea urchin, the sunflower star and a flat, thin fish called the big skate. Offshore swims the biggest animal of any on Earth: the 150-ton blue whale.

Waves travel thousands of miles across the Pacific Ocean, striking the coast with great force.

bigger sizes than it would in gentle waters.

Some animals depend on tough body parts, such as shells, to protect themselves. Others bend with the waves. Some lie low or hang on tightly so the water washes right over them. Others huddle together or hide among rocks.

A few animals combine ways of surviving. California blue mussels, for instance, protect themselves by clustering tightly in huge beds. Tough shells—up to 10 inches long—shield their soft bodies. Strong threads anchor these shells to shore but also bend, like elastic, with the waves. Gooseneck barnacles also protect themselves with tough shells. They use a strong glue to stick to rocks, and their flexible gooseneck "stalks" let them move with the water.

Certain plants, such as sea palms, grow very well here too. Looking like groves of tiny palm trees, they cling tightly to rocks along the wildest of coasts. After waves knock them flat, sea palms rise up again.

Wild waters also occur in narrow passages where changing tides produce very fast-flowing currents. The

Thick shells help protect gooseneck barnacles from rough water and predators.

Tube worms live inside tough, flexible tubes. When disturbed, they draw in their colorful feeding "plumes."

two fastest flows in the North Pacific — and the world — are through Sechelt Rapids and Nakwakto Rapids in British Columbia, where currents reach nearly 20 miles an hour.

There is more life in current-swept passages than anywhere else in the sea. Whole walls of rock are crowded with plants and animals — some living on top of one another. They all thrive on rich supplies of nutrients and oxygen delivered by the flows.

But, like sea life on the exposed coast, life in these passages must be able to survive the speed and strength of the water. Blue-clawed crabs tuck themselves inside empty shells of giant barnacles and filter food from passing water. Masses of feather-duster tube worms — 3 feet tall — poke only their red plumes out of leathery tubes to snag their meals. Three-foot-long finger sponges bend their rubbery bodies with the currents.

Different kinds of corals also thrive here, clustered protectively in colonies. Clumps of pink soft coral cover rocks, and basket stars, which look like knotted string, "tie" themselves to the coral. In deep, clear water in some passages, divers discovered a firm coral, a pink-and-white beauty that people didn't even know existed until the 1980s.

Exploring Underwater Worlds

People may be land animals, but they have adapted to the sea. With gear for scuba diving, they are able to swim like fish. Air tanks on their backs let them breathe underwater for up to an hour. Fins on their feet help them swim farther and faster with less work. And vests, called buoyancy control devices, act just like sacs of air in the bodies of fish: they help divers rise, sink or stay still in the water.

Scuba divers also wear masks, which trap air in front of their eyes, to help them see clearly. Some use special equipment so they can talk with other divers. And in the North Pacific, most divers put on

The Hidden Rainbow

Sea life is splattered with color: greens, reds, oranges, yellows, purples, pinks and blues. Yet even in clear water on sunny days, these colors are hard to see. Like a filter, water absorbs color from sunlight; red disappears completely within several feet of the surface. And the deeper the water, the more other colors are absorbed. That's why divers need artificial light — at all depths — to reveal the rainbow of color that is really beneath the sea.

drysuits to keep body heat in and cold water out. Underneath, they can wear their regular clothes.

People who don't dive can ride in tiny sports submarines built for two. These subs can move farther and faster than divers do. They have pockets of air in the cockpits so the pilot and passenger can breathe and talk normally.

If people want to explore water deeper than 100 feet, they need different equipment, such as deep-diving suits or larger submarines. Or they can

People suit up in scuba-diving gear to explore one of the world's most amazing seas: the coastal waters of the North Pacific.

stay at the surface and use robots, called ROVs — Remotely Operated Vehicles — to explore the sea. People direct an ROV and control where it moves, even thousands of feet down. They use its video camera to see what it "sees."

* * *

Exploring a sea brimming with life is always an adventure. Each trip underwater is a chance to enjoy something different, a chance to discover something new. From its quiet inlets to its fast-flowing passages, the coastal North Pacific is nothing less than a wonder world — one well worth exploring and well worth caring for, too.

Ocean Oddities

- One wave off Oregon was so strong it tossed a 132-pound rock 130 feet into the air.

- Thousands of herring travel so closely together they swim like a single, super-sized, silvery fish.

- The word "scuba" comes from SCUBA, which stands for Self-Contained Underwater Breathing Apparatus.

- Each year, gray whales swim between Alaska and Mexico, making one of the longest annual trips of any mammal on Earth.

- As young fish, flounders swim upright. Gradually, their skulls twist and their bodies tilt until they swim horizontally.

ROPOS for Research

Scientists who study the sea use scuba gear, submarines and ROVs to help them. One of the new ROVs used in North Pacific research is ROPOS, the Remotely Operated Platform for Ocean Science. Lowered from a ship by a long cable, ROPOS explores the sea to depths of 11,500 feet. Scientists operate it from controls aboard ship. They use the cameras and "arms" on ROPOS to do many things: map the sea floor, measure temperatures, search for objects and collect samples of animals, rocks and water.

Chapter Two

Plants of Plenty

It's possible to be surrounded by millions of plants but not see any. In the ocean, most plants are so tiny you need a microscope to look at them. But the sea also has plants that grow 100 feet in height, taller than many apartment buildings.

The coastal waters of the North Pacific are rich with plants — at least 600 different kinds. Their colors generally depend on how deep they grow. Plants near the surface are mostly green, but farther down they are mainly brown or gold. In the dim light of even deeper water, most plants are red.

Like land plants, sea plants use sunlight for energy to grow. Where it's too deep for light to reach, plants

Long, leaflike blades flutter above divers who swim through forests of tall bull kelp.

On most crabs, like this slender or
mud crab, the front legs take the
form of large claws.

don't live. Along most of the North Pacific coast, light needed for growth seldom reaches farther than 100 feet. But in a few places — where the water is very clear — plants grow in light 200 feet down.

Except for sea grasses, nearly all plants in the sea are algae: simple plants that have no roots, leaves or real stems. Algae that are big enough for the eye to see easily are called seaweeds.

Meadows for Crabs

Long, green sea grass grows well in North Pacific waters. Like land grass, it forms roots, leaves and plain, green flowers. But water, not air, carries pollen to flowers on sea grass. Many kinds of crabs, as well as jellyfish, small fish and other little sea animals, use this grass for food and shelter. They cling to the grass or hide among it. They nibble the leaves and lay their eggs on them. Seabirds also feed on sea grass and eat some of the animals that live in it.

One kind of grass, called eelgrass, puts down roots in sandy or muddy sea floors and grows as tall as 5 feet. Each plant produces three to six pale green leaves and nutlike seeds. In shallow, sheltered places, eelgrass often forms wide, green meadows. Besides attracting lots of animals, such as crabs and seabirds, eelgrass hosts other plants, which grow on its leaves.

In wind-blown water along rocky coasts, a shorter sea grass, called surfgrass, grows about 3 feet high. Its slender, bright green leaves shelter many kinds of small animals from ocean blasts. Little fish, snails and worms live along its roots as well as its leaves.

Forests for Fish

Picture a land forest of tall trees with ferns and bushes growing at their base. As branches sway in the wind, sunlight drifts to the forest floor. Birds flit about, and other small animals, from slugs to squir-

Grass That Isn't

Sometimes a single leaf breaks off a clump of eelgrass and drifts through the water. The "leaf" may not be a leaf at all, but a skinny, green fish. When this bay pipefish, as it is called, swims through the water, it holds its pencil-shaped body almost straight up and down. When it wants to rest, it settles among the eelgrass, where it blends right in. If the pipefish is a male, he may have his whole family with him. He carries hundreds of eggs in a long pouch on his underside until they hatch.

Kelp Help

Lots of animals use kelp, but human beings use it, too. For years, aboriginal people on the North Pacific coast gathered long, tough stalks to use as rope and fishing line. They also poured oil into the stalks and used them as containers. They even made balls for beach hockey by cutting and drying pieces of kelp.

Many people eat kelp and fertilize their gardens and fields with it. They use kelp to make hundreds of products, such as pudding, toothpaste and medicine. Kelp also is used to make paint smooth and thick and to keep crystals from forming in ice cream.

rels, search for food. Now and then, a large animal, such as a wolf, appears and stalks its next meal.

The sea has forests, too. Stands of tall, green-gold seaweed, such as bull kelp, can grow 100 feet high, while smaller seaweeds grow in the shadows. The long, leaflike blades of kelp flutter in ocean currents, letting in slivers of sunshine. Hundreds of fish of all colors flit through the forests, and seabirds dive into the water to snatch some. Many small animals, such as urchins and slugs, live and feed in kelp stands. Bigger animals, such as seals and sea otters, hunt in the forests and rest among the drifting blades. Even gray whales sometimes use kelp forests to hide their young from killer whales.

In the coastal waters of the North Pacific, undersea forests provide food, shelter and nurseries for sea life. Stands of bull kelp are among the most common, especially in fast-moving waters of exposed coasts. Tough, rootlike parts, called holdfasts, anchor them firmly to rocks on the sea floor.

During spring and summer, the thick, hollow stalks of bull kelp usually grow to their full height. At the top of each stalk, there's a gas-filled float—bigger than a man's fist. It acts like a balloon and lifts the kelp blades up toward the light. When fall comes, storms usually sweep these kelp giants away. But with the return of spring, the fast-growing forests rise again.

Soup for Whales

Thick, green soup. That's what the sea becomes when billions of algae grow in the water. Most of these plants are so tiny they have only one cell each. They are not anchored like seaweeds with holdfasts or like sea grasses with roots. These algae just float in the water, drifting with tides and currents. In a mass, they are called phytoplankton (*phyto* means plant and *plankton* means drifting). People

Red plants in deep
sea water use dim
sunlight for energy
to grow.

see them only as a green cloud in the water or, sometimes, as a film on the surface.

Although the plants that make up phytoplankton are very tiny, they are some of the most important plants on Earth. Together, they produce most of the world's oxygen. They are also the basis for most of the food in the sea. Many animals eat phytoplankton; other animals feed on these animals and so on—forming what is called a food chain. There are thousands of these chains in the sea.

Phytoplankton is also important to life on land. Many food chains in the sea link with food chains on land. For example, bald

In one of the sea's many food chains,
a sea star preys on a thick-shelled
snail called an abalone.

eagles eat gulls, which eat sea stars, which eat shellfish, which eat microscopic animals, which eat phytoplankton.

Some food chains are very long; others are very short. Surprisingly, huge whales, such as the blue whale and the gray whale, are part of very short food chains: they feed directly on masses of microscopic plants and tiny animals. These whales don't have to use lots of energy to catch their food. They can afford to be large.

* * *

Changes in sunlight, temperatures and winds affect the growth of sea plants, and so does pollution from industries, cities and ships. With so much depending on life in the ocean, people would do well to protect these important plants of plenty.

Soup and Seaweed Surprises

- More than 700 algae can live in a quart of sea water.

- The holdfast of one kind of seaweed, the perennial kelp, is so big it can seat two divers.

- Red seaweed lines floors and walls of some dimly lit caves beneath the sea.

- Water accounts for more than 80 percent of the weight of phytoplankton.

- Thick, purplish-pink "paint" spilled over rocks and shells in the sea is really a hard seaweed, called corallike algae.

Living Night Light

On moonless nights, waves glitter as they slap ships at sea, and trails of ship-plowed water glow a ghostly green. For centuries people wondered why, and many suggested supernatural causes. But the answer lies with microscopic ocean creatures that have traits of both plants and animals. When something, such as a ship, disturbs them, chemicals inside them react and produce a flash of light. Millions of these creatures, all flashing in the water, create a dazzling display—one of the oddest in the sea.

Chapter Three

Spineless Superstars

The octopus often takes a curious interest in divers and their scuba or photography equipment.

It's hard to believe that a wrinkly bag with eight arms is a real animal—let alone a smart one. But the giant Pacific octopus is very real, and full of surprises. It has the best-developed brain of all invertebrates (animals with no spines, or backbones). Researchers have discovered that the octopus can learn and remember; they think it may even be as smart as a cat.

Weighing up to 150 pounds and stretching 23 feet from arm to arm, the giant Pacific octopus is the biggest octopus in the world. But it doesn't harm people. In fact, divers welcome the chance to watch some of the amazing things it can do:

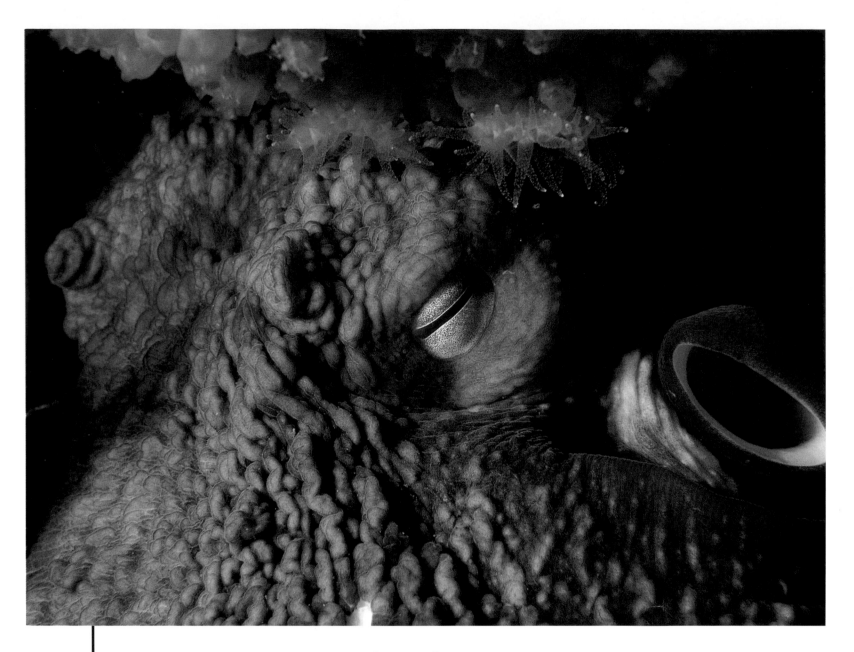

The octopus points its large siphon forward
or backward, shooting out water to propel
its body through the sea.

- make its skin bumpy or smooth to blend with the background;
- change color by opening and closing thousands of sacs beneath its skin;
- use the tips of its arms to pick up shells or sniff out food;
- scrape meat from a crab, using a tongue and a parrotlike beak;
- swim by taking in water and then squeezing it out again;
- pull itself across the sea floor, using more than 200 suction disks under each arm;
- create a screen of dark fluid so that it can escape unseen;
- stretch itself so thin it can squeeze its boneless body through a crack between rocks; and
- hang 150,000 grapelike eggs from the roof of its den (just the female does this).

The octopus is only one of thousands of animals without backbones in coastal North Pacific waters. Together, they form a group so various they include animals of almost every color, shape and behavior imaginable.

Tubes That Grab

Masses of "petals"—pink, white, red, purple, orange and green—quiver in the water. They blanket walls of rocks and floors of passages. They poke out of crevices and hang down from ledges. Although they bring beauty to underwater gardens, they are not flowers but tubelike animals with tentacles that grab prey. In size, these sea anemones range from the strawberry anemone—only three-quarters of an inch across—to the plumose anemone, which can grow more than ten times as wide.

Sea anemones attach themselves to hard objects, such as rocks, or build burrows in mud and sand. Some stay in one spot for up to thirty years, but they can glide on their bottoms if they need to. One

Holey Softy

Sponges are animals so simple they don't even look like living things. They don't have many body parts, not even mouths. But they have lots—even millions—of holes, called pores. Food and water flow into sponges through their smaller pores, and water flows back out through their larger ones. Sponges can be bigger than people or small enough to live on scallop shells. They add color to the sea and provide food and shelter for many animals. Not bad for a softy full of holes.

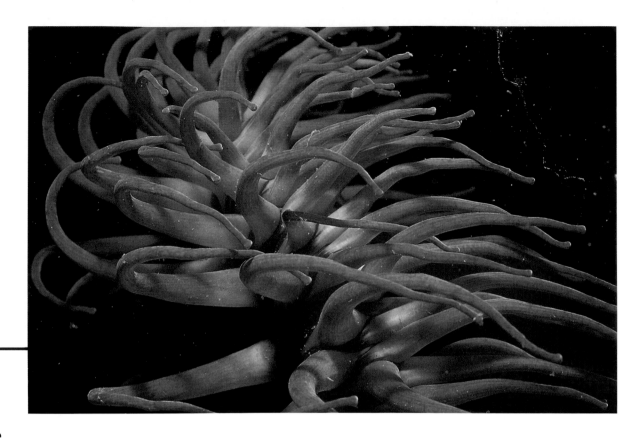

Growing up to 10 inches, the fish-eating sea anemone uses its colorful tentacles to catch small fish.

kind, called the swimming anemone, can thrash its way through water to escape predators, such as sea stars.

Sea anemones reproduce in different ways, including splitting in two. They may break off part of the base of their tube or tear themselves in half — top to bottom — and create a whole new anemone. The little surf anemone, or colonial anemone, is one kind that divides again and again, creating large colonies of anemones.

When one colony grows toward another, war may break out. The anemones beat each other using tiny clubs packed with stinging cells. Unless one of the colonies draws back, the anemones fight to the death. In the end, what is left between them is a bare strip of

22

The little stalked jellyfish attaches itself to eelgrass. Unlike bell-shaped jellyfish, it has eight arms with tentacles that capture food.

rock—a peace zone—that neither colony can enter without starting another war.

Sea anemones are not the only colorful, tubelike creatures in the sea. Thousands of polyps—tiny animals that look like miniature anemones—join together in beautiful colonies of coral. Some kinds of colonies have soft, spongelike skeletons; others are stiff enough to form shapes, such as fans.

Looking like coral polyps or sea anemones flipped upside down, jellyfish float in the sea. They drift with the currents and swim slowly by squeezing and relaxing their bodies. They use tentacles around their tubelike bodies to capture food. One of the biggest jellyfish in the coastal North Pacific is the sea blubber. Its body is 2 feet across and its tentacles are up to 8 feet long.

Slugs Deluxe

Most backyard slugs are plain animals, without much variety in shape or color. But in the sea, many slugs are dazzling. There are many different kinds—in different shades and designs. In size, they range from three-quarters of an inch to about 12 inches.

These slugs are called nudibranchs (pronounced "noo-di-branks"), which means "naked gills," because their gills stick out as decorative bumps and spikes on their backs. Eye-catching colors and shapes protect nudibranchs. They are the slug's way of saying: "Don't eat me. I taste bad."

The names of many kinds of nudibranchs describe what they look like. There's the orange-peel nudibranch, a 12-inch giant that is one of the biggest nudibranchs in the world; the tiny hooded nudibranch, which throws its hood to catch floating sea life; and the Spanish shawl, a purple beauty with bright orange tips and red feelers on its head.

The shaggy mouse nudibranch is an ocean slug that often makes its home in beds of eelgrass.

But the strangest nudibranch is one that can swim from predators, such as large sea stars. Called the giant nudibranch, it twists its 10-inch-long body back and forth until its two ends nearly meet. It can't swim very far or very long, but it can usually swim enough to escape.

The giant nudibranch has an odd way of feeding. It favors a type of sea anemone that lives in a tube of mucus and sand. When the anemone pokes out its tentacles to catch food, the nudibranch tries to grab some tentacles in its jaws. The anemone draws back into its tube, sometimes pulling the head of the nudibranch with it. It's not as gruesome as it sounds. After the nudibranch eats, it yanks itself out unharmed and the anemone grows new tentacles.

Creatures with Crust

Unlike soft-bodied slugs, octopuses and sea anemones, some sea life comes wrapped in a hard crust. It's actually a skeleton or shell, which animals such as crabs, shrimps and barnacles wear on the outsides of their bodies. The shell of a crab can be smooth, hairy or spiny. When the ever-growing crab gets too big for its shell, the shell splits and the crab slips out the back. Soon after, a new, larger shell hardens over its body.

Most crabs don't swim. They just walk around the sea floor — usually sideways — on four pairs of legs. Up front, they have two strong, snapping pincers for fighting, climbing and catching food.

One of the biggest crabs in the coastal North Pacific is the Puget Sound king crab. More than 12 inches across, it looks like an armored tank, blending well with the rocks it hunts among. The smaller decorator crab dresses up its crusty covering so it can hide: it clips bits of seaweed and sponge and puts them on its back. Little hairs with hooks keep these bits from falling off.

The huge Puget Sound king crab grows a thick, bumpy covering. Sometimes it further protects itself by folding its legs under its body, forming a hard "box."

The hermit crab doesn't have a crust that covers its whole body. Its soft rear end is naked, so the crab sticks it into an empty snail shell. As the hermit crab grows, it moves to larger and larger shells.

Unlike crabs, shrimps wear thin, often see-through shells. They scoot about in the water, using fanlike tails to shoot backward and five pairs of legs to walk or jump forward. Several kinds of shrimps change their sex, from male to female, as they age. Striped with neon blue and yellow, the colorful clown shrimp is one of the most attractive. It often lives and feeds among sea anemones, unharmed by their stinging tentacles.

The clown shrimp often lives with
crimson sea anemones, eating bits
of food they drop or discard.

Barnacles produce the hardest crust of all — but only after they stick themselves to rocks, wharfs, ships and other animals, such as crabs and whales. Before that, the barnacle is free-roaming, like the shrimp. It goes through several stages before it glues its head to an object and forms a tough crust, or shell. After that, the barnacle pokes only its feathery feet into the water so it can kick food into its mouth.

Rock Stars

Lots of animals with spiny skin, such as sea stars, sea urchins and sea cucumbers, live among rocks on sea floors. Most sea stars have five arms, but some, like the huge sunflower star, have up to twenty-four arms. Hundreds of tube-shaped feet are attached to the undersides of these arms. But many feet don't help sea stars move fast. The speediest takes about a minute to travel about 3 feet.

In fact, sea star feet are more helpful in feeding than in walking. Many sea stars use them, like suction cups, to clamp onto mussels and clams while they pull the shells open a crack. Then the stars turn their stomachs inside out, poke them out through their mouths and squeeze them between the shells. They start digesting shellfish right in their shells and may not finish for two to three days.

Sea urchins also use their tube feet to help them feed. The feet catch bits of seaweed drifting in water and they also hold onto growing seaweed while the urchins nibble it. Beneath their bodies, sea urchins

The mouths of sea stars, such as this cookie sea star, are in the middle of their bodies, on the undersides.

The long, prickly spines of the red sea urchin — a favorite food of wolf-eels and sea otters — are red, pink or purple.

each have five sharp teeth that never stop growing. Some kinds, such as purple sea urchins, use these teeth and their long, pointed spines to grind cubbyholes in rock or cement pilings. Then the urchins snuggle into these holes for safety. Some also shield themselves with pebbles and tiny shells, which their feet hold against their bodies.

The sea cucumber looks a bit like the vegetable of the same name, except for its feet — usually arranged in five long rows. The cucum-

ber uses these feet to move slowly across the sea floor. About the only time it speeds up is when predators, such as sea stars, appear. Then it may arch back and forth, trying to escape.

Some kinds of sea cucumbers tuck themselves between rocks to feed on bits of floating food. They use their tube feet to hold themselves in place and tentacles around their mouths to grab food. After eating all summer, they may throw up their innards to get rid of par-

Life in the Graveyard

Wild winds and waves have created a watery graveyard of ships along the North Pacific coast. Some of these wrecks are more than 200 years old, and many lie in pieces on the ocean floor. Other wrecks have held together — at least in chunks — and gained new life as underwater reefs. Gradually, they became encrusted with colorful sponges, giant barnacles, feathery tube worms, bright corals and fluffy sea anemones. Sea stars, crabs and octopuses moved in. Jellyfish swam through, and many kinds of fish, including sharks, began hunting right on board.

asites — plants or animals that are feeding on them. Sometimes they also throw up their innards to puzzle predators. Then these cool cucumbers grow new ones.

* * *

About 95 percent of all animals on Earth are creatures without backbones. They have important roles to play in nature. But scientists are concerned that some kinds are disappearing because people abuse them or pollute their homes.

Learning a bit about these animals is the first step to appreciating them. Let's hope people soon learn to appreciate spineless superstars for what they really are.

Sea Critter Quirks

- A spiny pink scallop sees with rows of tiny eyes found on the flesh along the edges of both its shells. The scallop swims by opening and closing these shells very fast.

- Algae that live inside giant green anemones gain a safe home; in return, they produce oxygen and sugars that the anemones use. They also give the anemones a green color.

- Hard, overlapping plates protect the armored sea cucumber, which looks like a vegetable cut in half from end to end.

- If a crab loses a leg or a claw, it can grow a new one. Sea stars can replace lost arms; some kinds also grow more arms as they get older.

- Some nudibranchs use the stinging cells in sea anemone tentacles by taking them into their own bodies for defense.

The spiny pink scallop, which usually
rests on the sea floor, swims away
when it senses an octopus or sea star.

Chapter Four

Far-Out Fish

The big male lingcod guards the eggs he fertilizes.

Fish may not smell good but they certainly smell well. Their nostrils—which have nothing to do with breathing—work full-time at sniffing out things. Sharks smell blood in water more than 1,300 feet away. Tidepool sculpins smell their way back to their own pools after waves wash them out.

Although many fish don't hear as well as people, most see better than people in dim light. They have a keen sense of taste, which is closely linked with their sense of smell. Some even use body parts besides their mouths—such as whiskers on their snouts—to taste-test food before they eat.

Along the sides of many fish, nerves join strings of

The Mystery of the Sixgills

One of the most mysterious fish of the North Pacific coast is the sixgill shark, whose ancestors swam the seas millions of years ago. Although it lives around the world — often in water as deep as 5,000 feet — it rises to within 30 feet of the surface around Vancouver Island, British Columbia. For reasons nobody knows, this is the only place on Earth that the sixgill surfaces regularly. Although it can grow to more than 10 feet in length, it seems to feed on small animals, such as crabs and little fish.

cells that sense slight changes in water pressure. These strings, called lateral lines, help fish swim closely together without bumping into one another and warn them of predators approaching. By sensing the strength of different currents, some fish use these lines to find their way through the sea.

Fish have much in common, but each kind has special features, too. Among the more than 450 different kinds of fish in the coastal waters of the North Pacific, some are so unusual, so comical or so lovely that they barely seem real.

Fish in Coats, Fish in Armor

Most fish produce slime that protects them from scrapes and infection. Slime also makes fish watertight and helps them slip easily through water. But as slime producers, few fish equal the Pacific hagfish — also called the slime eel. When it's disturbed, the hagfish oozes milky-colored slime from pores all along its body. In no time, it is wrapped completely in a thick coat so slippery nothing can grab it.

The trouble is that the same slimy coat that protects the hagfish from predators can smother it. But the hagfish is an amazing escape artist. It twists about to tie its soft, wormlike body into a knot. Then it rubs the slime off by pulling itself — from tail to head — through the knot. Having no bones makes it possible for the fish to do this trick.

Fins, scales, eyes, jaws and a stomach are some of the other things the hagfish doesn't have. It is one of the most primitive fish on Earth. But it has survived millions of years — in its own way. The hagfish can live months without food. When it's hungry, it searches for prey by swimming like a snake. It can sense only light and darkness with eyespots on its head, but it uses smell and touch to find meals of sick, dead or trapped fish.

Fleshy growths on its head help the hagfish feel its way about.

With a tongue that is covered with hornlike teeth, the hagfish burrows into its prey—often through openings, such as gill slits or the anus. Then it eats the insides of the fish, leaving only a shell of skin and bones. One long intestine, which runs from the throat to the back end of the hagfish, does most of the digesting.

Unlike the hagfish, most fish are covered with scales that protect their bodies and grow as they grow. But sharks are fish with a unique covering: a rough and tough skin of toothlike scales, called denticles. Built like real teeth—even coated with hard enamel—these denticles cover the entire body of most sharks. They form a flexible armor that protects the shark and reduces drag when it swims. In fact, researchers are testing coverings designed like shark skin for use on boats.

The fancy "hat" of the decorated warbonnet blends in well with many kinds of seaweed.

Sharks never stop growing, so their denticles—and the teeth in their mouths—are always being replaced with larger ones. Denticles and teeth that are lost or broken are also replaced, keeping sharks in top shape as predators.

But these swift-swimming tanks of teeth have a reputation they don't deserve. Unlike sharks that star in movies, they do not especially hunt people. Most just eat what's handy and what their teeth—which range from big spikes to tiny hooks—can manage.

The spiny dogfish is the most common shark along the North Pacific coast. Only about 5 feet long, it eats food such as small fish, worms and squid. It may swim quietly beside a diver or travel in a school with a thousand other dogfish. Its rough, denticle-covered skin is sometimes used as sandpaper.

The basking shark—the world's second-largest fish—grows to 50 feet in length, but its teeth are tiny. That's because it feeds on very small plants and animals, which it filters from water. The only ways the basking shark might harm people are accidental: a scrape from its sharp, pointed denticles or a bump from its buslike body.

Fish with Hats, Fish with Buttons

On shallow sea floors, red-brown warbonnets tuck themselves between rocks and poke their heads into seaweed. There they blend in perfectly, thanks to their "hats"—several fluffy stalks of flesh that look just like seaweed. The mosshead warbonnet has a flat

The ancient sixgill shark swims slowly, but it can burst through the water for short distances.

The big head and piglike snout of the little grunt sculpin account for one of its other names: pigfish.

hat: many stalks about the same height. Its larger cousin, the decorated warbonnet, has a taller hat of uneven stalks. Although warbonnets are hard to see, they are always ready to dash off, if spotted, and find a different place to hide.

Another sea floor fish, the midshipman, has no need for hats, but it uses "buttons" to signal other fish, especially a mate. Rows of spots along its head and body gleam like the brass buttons on the jacket of a midshipman (a naval student). Tiny light cells in the skin make up these spots, and the fish can turn them on and off when it wants to.

40

The midshipman is also called the singing fish because it is one of the noisiest fish in the sea. It hums, grunts, squeaks and whistles to attract mates and to let other fish know when they are in its territory.

Fish That Walk, Fish That Fly

What fish do most is swim. But colorful, big-headed fish, called sculpins, also "walk." Their side fins are fan-shaped, with fingerlike points that sculpins use to prop themselves up and walk across the sea floor.

One of the smallest sculpins is the grunt. It's only 3 inches long and gets its name from the sound it makes when handled. Divers often see a striped grunt sculpin peeking out of an empty bottle, large shell or crack in a rock where it hides. Sometimes it uses its wide fins to hop, instead of walk.

The red Irish lord is a much larger sculpin and a big eater. It is also one of the brightest, most beautiful fish in the sea, but that doesn't make it easy to spot. The red Irish lord just nestles among rocks covered with equally colorful plants, sponges and anemones and stays very still. Until it walks or swims, most predators don't even notice it.

The prize for the oddest sculpin goes to the sad-faced sailfin. Thick, black lines, like clown makeup, streak across its cheeks. When the sailfin sculpin is resting, the front part of its top fin stands up straight, looking like a mast on a sailboat. But when it swims or walks, the sculpin usually lowers its "mast."

To swim, most fish depend on their strong tails, which propel them by swishing back and forth. But some fish, such as skates, have only little tails, so they swim by "flying." Skates are flattened fish with side fins large enough to look and act like wings. When skates sweep gracefully through water, they just let their narrow, whiplike tails flow behind.

Aliens from Another Sea

Some years, changes in winds and ocean currents near the equator cause warm water to flow up the coast to the North Pacific. This event, called El Niño, often brings strange visitors with it — such as the razor-toothed barracuda. Strong and sleek, this fish is a speed demon. It not only cruises very fast, it uses stored energy and special tail muscles to bolt — like lightning — after its prey. In short bursts, the barracuda can race through water at speeds of 60 miles an hour.

The big skate, which often presses itself against sandy sea floors, cannot take in water through its mouth. Instead, it uses openings near its eyes.

Skates usually fly just above the sea floor. When they rest, they lie on sand or gravel, often burying themselves in it. Their skin is a sandy color, so when they are still, they are almost invisible. Divers and predators can swim by without even seeing the world's largest skate, a fish more than 6 feet long and 200 pounds in weight.

Fish That Share, Fish That Eggsit

Among most kinds of fish, males and females spend little time together, but wolf-eels are an exception. The brownish female and gray-colored male share the same territory and the same den for life. They also share the work of guarding the eggs the female lays. But what a couple they make: two huge heads crammed with wolflike teeth and blotchy, eel-like bodies up to 6 feet long.

As fierce as they look, wolf-eels are usually slow-moving, gentle fish. They not only share a home with each other, they also share it with rockfish, which are much smaller. When a wolf-eel is eating, one or two rockfish often hover nearby, nibbling any bits that float away.

Many wolf-eels approach divers who hand-feed them a favorite food: sea urchins. They also seem to enjoy being rubbed and stroked. A pair that are comfortable with people often circle divers with their bodies, pressing against them for attention.

Among the many kinds of fish that don't live with a mate, there are several that leave eggsitting duties to the males. One example is the spotted, green-brown lingcod. It's a big, aggressive fish, up to 5 feet long. And, like the wolf-eel, it has huge, wolflike teeth. The female lingcod lays half a million eggs among sea-bottom rocks, then leaves, and the male moves in to guard the mass. Taking his job very seriously, he lunges at anything that comes close. He even attacks animals bigger than himself.

A much smaller fish, the male threespine stickleback not only guards his eggs, but builds a nest for them. Using gluelike liquid from his body, he sticks seaweed together. Then he rubs against it to shape the nest like a tube. When the liquid hardens, the nest is strong and ready for a female to lay her eggs in it. The male fertilizes the eggs and then brings in more females — one by one — until the nest is full of eggs. After that, he guards the eggs until they hatch.

* * *

People are one of the most efficient predators of fish. Commercial fishing crews use computers, radar and underwater cameras to help

Look Who's Fishing

Fish have many kinds of predators — even some that come from shore. Great blue herons stand like statues in the water and then strike in a flash, their long beaks snapping up some passing fish. Raccoons scoot along the shore, using their handlike front paws to grab fish and other sea life from the shallows. Big black bears also lumber to the water to fish. They may even wade right in — especially where a river meets the sea. With lightning speed, they slap a paw over a fish and then press it to the bottom or fling it to shore. Or they use their strong jaws to snap a fish right from the water.

A pair of wolf-eels make loyal mates.
The female (left) is usually much darker
in color than the male (right).

capture large numbers of food fish, such as herring and salmon. But overfishing has harmed these fish populations. Canada and the United States have been trying to protect them by setting limits on catches. They are also working to save and improve fish habitat.

Fabulous Fish Feats

- A single shark can lose — and replace — 30,000 teeth during its lifetime.

- Most kinds of rockfish give birth to live young. They are often more than twenty years old before they reproduce.

- The Pacific hagfish has four hearts, each beating at its own pace.

- The colorful blackeye goby lives in shallow water, where it eats shrimp; yet its cousin, the bay goby, is so small that it shares a burrow with a mud shrimp.

- The female midshipman attaches her eggs to the undersides of rocks. When they hatch, the young fish stay attached to these rocks for a few weeks.

One of the tallest birds along the North Pacific coast, the great blue heron stands 5 feet tall. Its favorite food is fish.

otters rarely leave it. In all, about thirty different kinds of marine mammals live in the coastal North Pacific.

One thing they all have in common is a big appetite. In these cold waters, mammals need a lot of food to produce a lot of heat. And they need to build thick layers of fat to keep in the heat and store energy. Lighter than water, this fat also helps marine mammals float.

Mammals That Blow Their Tops

Unlike most animals, whales have holes in the tops of their heads. These blowholes stay closed, except when the whales come to the surface. There

To check what's happening above water, the gray whale spyhops: it "stands" on end so its tiny eyes can peek out.

the whales blow hot, stale air out of their lungs and grab quick, fresh breaths. Then they close their blowholes before diving again.

Some whales have only one blowhole; others have two. Those with one also have teeth. Except for the big sperm whale, one-hole whales are the smaller kinds, such as killer whales, dolphins and porpoises. Instead of teeth, whales with two blowholes have baleen — hundreds of long, bristly plates that hang from their upper jaws. Both the gray whale and the humpback whale are baleen whales.

What whales have in their mouths determines what they eat and, in part, how they behave. Toothed whales must swim fast to chase after prey, such as fish, squid and small mammals. These whales often hunt in groups, which means they need to "talk" with one another. They squeal, squeak, whistle and make several other sounds. They also make clicking noises and then listen to their echoes to judge how big and how far away something is. This echolocation, as it's called, helps whales find their prey.

The killer whale, or orca, hunts in families, called pods. Members use the special language of each pod to talk to other members of their family. They also make sirenlike noises to talk to killer whales in other pods.

Unlike toothed whales, most baleen whales are big and swim slowly, filtering tiny plants and animals and small fish from the water. The bristly edges of their baleen plates snag the food; then the tongue scrapes it off and throws it back to the throat. Some of these whales eat tons of food every day, but they don't need help from other whales to get it. They spend less time in groups and generally "talk" less than toothed whales.

Most baleen whales feed near the surface of the sea, but the gray whale heads to the bottom to eat. One of its favorite foods — tiny animals called amphipods — burrow into the sea floor. They are so small

Songs the Humpback Sings

Male humpback whales are famous for their songs. They sing the loudest, longest, most complicated songs of any whale on Earth. Hour after hour, the humpbacks repeat patterns of moans and sighs, chirps and squeaks. All male humpbacks in the same area sing much the same songs — mainly to attract females or to warn away other males. Every year, the songs change slightly. Although the humpbacks sing most in their warm breeding waters, scientists think they also sing as they migrate between Hawaii and Alaska.

49

The harbor seal basks in warm sunshine on shore, but if disturbed, it is quick to plunge back into the sea.

that 100 million of them weigh only as much as one gray whale. To eat amphipods and other small creatures, the whale sucks in mouthfuls of sea floor, then strains out the mud and sand and swallows its prey.

Mammals with Legless Feet

Of all marine mammals, the pinnipeds — seals, sea lions and fur seals — spend the most time on land. That's where they rest, bask in the sun and give birth. But pinnipeds don't have legs to help them get around. Their flattened "feet," or flippers, are attached directly to their bodies. That makes it hard for them to raise themselves enough to waddle.

Seashores and small islands on the North Pacific coast frequently come alive with the big, burly bodies of Steller's and California sea lions.

A mother sea otter takes constant care of her pup. She usually gives birth just once in two years.

Seals depend mostly on their body muscles to move across land. Sea lions and fur seals use their longer, stronger front flippers to raise their heads and shoulders. Then they turn their back flippers beneath their bodies and walk awkwardly on all fours.

But in the sea, pinnipeds become creatures of speed and grace. Hind flippers jet-propel seals through the water; front flippers power sea lions and fur seals. The layers of fat and heavy skin, which hinder them on land, help pinnipeds stay warm and float in the water.

Although pinnipeds have much in common, each one has its own ways too. The quiet harbor seal often spends its days alone or in small groups, but seems curious about people. It hangs around fishing docks to snap up scraps. Sometimes it trails divers through kelp, usually keeping far enough behind to stay out of reach.

The northern elephant seal is the largest pinniped in these waters. It shares two features with the elephant: a huge body and a long nose. A male weighs up to nearly 2 tons and his nose dangles about 12 inches beneath his mouth. When he wants to scare other males—especially at mating times—he fills his big nose with air. Then he curves it so the end points into his mouth. As he snorts, the sound bounces around in his mouth, growing so loud that it can be heard more than half a mile away.

Steller's and California sea lions are smaller than the elephant seal, but they are noisy too—both in and out of the water. People see sea lions most often in winter, when these pinnipeds leave the exposed coast and move to sheltered bays. There they clamber up on rocks and floating log booms, loudly announcing: "We're back." California sea lions—like toothed whales—also make noises in deep water to find fish by echolocation.

Next to the sea otter, the gray-brown northern fur seal has the thickest coat of any animal in North Pacific coastal waters. But divers and people on shore rarely see it. Migrating each year between Alaska and California, the fur seal often stays more than 10 miles off the coast.

Mammals That Hammer and Comb

Only one marine mammal can use a tool and that's the sea otter. Its back feet are webbed, but its front legs are equipped with paws. It uses them like hands to pick things up. When it dives underwater to gather food, such as sea urchins and clams, the otter also grabs a small rock. Then it tucks all these things into flaps of loose skin in its "armpits" and heads for the surface.

Floating on its back, the sea otter breaks into its catch by striking it with the rock. Or it may place the rock on its chest and bang the clams and urchins against it—like cracking eggs on a bowl. The "tap, tap, tap" and the smell of food attract hungry gulls and fish.

Just Playing Around

Sea lions love to play—especially in water. Spinning and swooping, several of them burst into action. They chase, they race. They flip upside down and blow bubbles. And they tease: one sea lion charges another at full-speed and then, at the last second, swerves to one side. Or one snatches a piece of kelp and flicks it at another—only to have a third sea lion pop between them and grab the kelp.

Keepers of the Forest

Every day the sea otter eats food that weighs one-quarter as much as its own body, and it likes to eat red sea urchins best. In its lifetime, a sea otter can eat enough of these urchins to turn its teeth and bones pink. That's a good thing for kelp forests. Urchins eat so much kelp that they can destroy a forest, removing all the seaweed and creating what scientists call an urchin barrens. Where sea otters control the number of red sea urchins, kelp forests thrive. So do all the plants and animals that live and hunt in them.

There are always scraps when the sea otter feeds. Every thirty seconds or so, it clutches its rock and prey and rolls in the water, washing away bits of food and shell. It makes sure its coat stays clean so the hairs trap air close to the skin. That helps the otter keep dry, warm and afloat.

The sea otter spends about half its life eating or grooming. It scrubs with its paws and combs its fur with its claws. It blows air into its coat and turns somersaults to wash and puff out its fur.

After a female gives birth, she spends a lot of time feeding, washing and grooming her pup. She cradles it on her chest, combs its fur and makes soft cooing sounds. If she senses any danger, she grasps the pup in her paws and dives underwater.

The only time a mother leaves her pup alone is when she gathers food. Then she floats the pup on its back, sometimes wrapping it in kelp so it won't drift. Still, the pup usually cries while she is gone.

When sea otters sleep, they often form a raft, a floating group of up to thirty otters, all of the same sex. They lie on their backs with their not-so-furry limbs poking out of the cold water. That helps to keep these limbs warm. Sometimes the otters wrap themselves in strong kelp blades so they are anchored while sleeping.

Unlike whales and pinnipeds, the sea otter is one of a kind in the ocean. Its relatives, such as the smaller river otters, are mainly land animals.

* * *

For many years, people ruthlessly killed marine mammals for their fur, blubber or baleen. Populations plunged; sea otters completely disappeared along much of the North Pacific coast; and the Pacific manatee became extinct. Then, in the 1900s, countries started to protect marine mammals from overhunting and biologists brought in sea otters from other places.

Between 1950 and the 1990s, the number of gray whales grew from a few hundred to about 18,000. But other sea mammals haven't done as well. Few will likely ever reach the populations they once had. But if people respect their needs, these mind-boggling mammals will always have a place on the North Pacific coast.

Mammal Magic

- A mother killer whale matches her breathing to her infant's. They open and close their blowholes at exactly the same times.

- An elephant seal can dive 4,000 feet to catch rays, sharks and other fish.

- During mating seasons, male fur seals can last three months without eating. They live on the energy stored as fat.

- The Dall's porpoise hunts at speeds of nearly 35 miles per hour.

- Sea otter fur is very dense: 650,000 hairs per square inch.

The Pacific white-sided dolphin is an ocean acrobat. In seconds, it leaps out of the water, flips onto its back and turns a dozen somersaults.

Index

DATE			